AS YOU WAIT...

A 21 day Devotional on waiting on the Lord

Pastor Joyce

you are blessed

Chris

2019

CONTENTS

As You Wait...

A 21 Day Devotional on Waiting on the Lord

ISBN: 978-1-913218-67-6

Author: Chido Madziko

Cover Design by Ncore Designs UK

Layout & Design by Loulita gill Design

ACKNOWLEDGEMENTS

I give God thanks and all the glory for enabling me and giving me the opportunity to write this Devotional on waiting on The Lord. All the wisdom, understanding and knowledge comes from Him and Him alone.

To my mum and my late dad, Mr & Mrs Isaac Nyasha Madziko, thank you for raising me to become the woman that I am today. You have always encouraged me that I can do anything.

To my sisters Reason & Junior, my brothers Munyaradzi & Nyasha, thank you for your love and support.

To my spiritual parents, Archbishop Climate & Dr Jennifer Irungu, thank you for running with the vision because it is through serving your vision that my vision was conceived and birthed. Thank you for your prayers, support and all the teachings. Truly the Kingdom Church is a place of strong spiritual growth and powerful blessings. Extending my special thanks also to the Kingdom Church family.

To my Uncle/ Father figure Pastor Brian Mujuru & my Auntie/ Advisor Minister Agatha, words are not enough to express my gratitude towards you. Thank you from the bottom of my heart for embracing me as my your own. Thank you for your love, prayers and the support you have given me. God bless you always.

To my mentor Mrs Vonayi Nyamazana, you are the midwife who has helped me birth this Devotional. Thank you with all my heart, for your support, love, prayers, and for pushing me out of my comfort zone. You're God sent. God bless you.

Special thanks to your husband Mr Mike Nyamazana & your children.

INTRODUCTION

I give God all the glory for enabling me and giving me the opportunity to write this Devotional on *"Waiting on God"*. I thank Him for all the people He has put in my life, who have helped me to discover the hidden treasure of writing that God had put in me.

The reason why I chose to write about waiting on God is to encourage someone who has been between a hard place and a rock. Someone who is in a situation where they have no power to do anything to change their situation. Or someone who has done all they can in their own power to change their situation but it only seems to get worse. This is where I come in and say, AS YOU WAIT ... WAIT ON GOD!

Waiting is hard! Let's be honest, no one likes to wait! And I am sure all of us can testify to the fact that we struggle with waiting! We want things done like yesterday! Sure enough God gives us these desires for different reasons, but the longer it takes for them to manifest, the more we become impatient. We start comparing ourselves with others and start to think that other people's lives are better than ours. The more we do these things the more we water down our faith in God. Our trust in Him starts to waiver and as a result we try to handle these challenges by ourselves which is never a good idea. We only end up in more of a mess than we were in before.

When I was growing up I never saw myself as a writer. I never thought that I would write anything, let alone write a Devotional that could help others. What I do know is that since I was little I have always loved reading. Then almost 3 years ago my uncle, (Pastor Brian Mujuru,) asked me to write a short Daily Devotional on his Facebook page every day to encourage people. At first I was dreading it; I mean truth be told I didn't want to do it, I was thinking, *"why can't he do it himself?"* Obviously I agreed to do it (I had no choice), but oh boy was he strict! I had to write and post every single day at a specific time, (no lateness was allowed)! But I am glad now that I accepted the challenge because even though I didn't understand why I had to do it, God did. Now I realise that it was a training ground for the greater that was to come. Even though I didn't have much revelation and depth to my writing then, it pushed me to read more material, listen to more teachings and bit by bit my roots of wisdom, understanding and knowledge started to grow and get deeper and stronger. As I kept on writing and as time went by I realised that I enjoyed the writing so much so that when he told me to stop I was actually disappointed.

Since that time I found myself praying for a writing ministry. I didn't know how it would come about or what I would write about. But I knew that I loved encouraging others; I am a very optimistic person. Then my auntie, (Minister Agatha Mujuru), introduced me to my now mentor, Mrs Vonayi Nyamazana, (and surprise surprise I didn't want to do it!) But she pushed me (she has been my advisor, auntie, mother and everything else), and I am very thankful to her because as soon as I took that step of faith and went to see her only God knew what was about to be birthed.

When I began my mentorship program my mentor asked me about some of the things I like to do and I told her that one of the things I love to do is writing. And since I have been waiting on God and believing God for a lot of things to take place in my life she advised me to write

Facebook posts, (yes back to Facebook posts again), encouraging someone who is in an exact situation as I am. But this time there was a different feeling to it; there was excitement and anticipation about what I was going to write. As I started doing that and as I continued praying for my writing ministry I actually saw a vision of books in front of me. And days after seeing that vision my mentor said, *"Chido I would like you to write a Devotional on waiting on God."* I give special thanks to Mrs Vonayi Nyamazana because God truly called her for such a time. It's not like she wasn't part of my life, she was there all along, but I believe that God called her this time especially to be a midwife who will help birth this particular Devotional. I got so motivated about writing that I jumped straight into it because I knew that this is a calling from God. And I give special thanks to my spiritual parents Archbishop Climate Irungu and Dr Jennifer Irungu for their prayers, guidance and especially their teaching. They have taught me that it doesn't matter who you are or where you come from, as long as you believe, God can enable you to do anything and everything, and through you God can do great and mighty things. I have been sitting at their feet for a while now and I can truly say that my writing ministry was conceived in the Kingdom Church.

As I began to write this Devotional I realised that God had already deposited what to write inside of me through my own personal journey of waiting on Him. I have had to hold on to God through prayer when nothing else makes sense, listening to teachings and reading other people's Devotionals. And truly God has drawn me to Himself.

Waiting on God is worth it! It's not easy, but it's worth it! And my message to all of you waiting on certain things to happen in your life is that: as you wait on God, you don't have to wait in misery! The devil would love for you to be miserable but don't give him the satisfaction; remember it's not about reaching your destination but about enjoying the journey to your destination! The Holy Spirit of God will give you love, joy and peace and your faith in God will grow. Remember that faith is the currency of Heaven and without faith it is impossible to please God. God will bring you to your promised land; AS YOU WAIT ... WAIT ON GOD!

PERSONAL DAILY CONFESSION!

I am strong in the Lord and in the power of His might. I put on the whole armor of God that I may be able to stand against the wiles of the devil. For we do not wrestle against flesh and blood, but against principalities, against powers, against the rulers of the darkness of this age, against spiritual hosts of wickedness in the heavenly places. Therefore I take up the whole armor of God, that I may be able to withstand in the evil day, and having done all, to stand.

I stand therefore, having girded my waist with truth, having put on the breastplate of righteousness, and having shod my feet with the preparation of the gospel of peace; above all, taking the shield of faith with which I will be able to quench all the fiery darts of the wicked one. And I take the helmet of salvation, and the sword of the Spirit, which is the word of God; praying always with all prayer and supplication in the Spirit. *"For though we walk in the flesh, we do not war according to the flesh. For the weapons of our warfare are not carnal but mighty in God for pulling down strongholds, casting down arguments and every high thing that exalts itself against the knowledge of God, bringing every thought into captivity to the obedience of Christ,"* (Ephesians 6:10-18, II Corinthians 10:3-5 NKJV).

Chapter One

WHAT DOES IT MEAN TO WAIT ON THE LORD?

IT MEANS THAT AS YOU WAIT ... YOU ARF: TRUSTING GOD!

I believe that waiting on God is to put your trust completely, 100% on God. To have your faith so grounded in God that there is no room to move to the left or to the right. That no matter what comes your way; *rain, fire, sunshine, hailstones, snow, thunder and lightning you believe that even though you walk through the valley of the shadow of death, you fear no evil, God is with you! (Psalm 23, Isaiah 43:1, 2)*

ALLOWING THE HOLY SPIRIT TO HELP YOU!

Truth be told, we're born impatient; we want everything right now. We want to understand things, situations, and circumstances now! Our minds can't stand waiting. And that is why most of the time people end up doing things that will hurt them either in the short run or long run because they allow their minds to control them. Don't allow your mind to control you, you can control your mind; the Holy Spirit can help you to do that! And when the Holy Spirit helps you, you will enjoy the waiting, because as you wait the Holy Spirit will begin to open up your understanding to a lot of things. You will begin to see things that you would never have seen or taken notice of before. Be best friends with the Holy Spirit of the living God.

BEING STILL AND KNOWING THAT GOD IS GOD!

Being still means you have ceased from following your own agenda or ingenuity; *you have stopped trusting in your own strength and will power. You are waiting upon the Lord to trade your weakness for His strength. (2 Corinthians 12:9).* Waiting on the Lord is not just ordinary waiting, where you just sit around doing nothing, letting time pass by until the time comes for you to get whatever it is you're waiting for! It involves being at rest in the Lord. Your attitude especially is very vital to your breakthrough. You cannot afford to complain and grumble; the children of Israel missed out on the Promised Land because they complained and grumbled against God. The word wait in the Bible carries the idea of confident expectation and hope. *"For God alone my soul waits in silence . . . my hope is from him" (Psalm 62:1, 5, ESV).* To wait upon the Lord is to expect something from Him in godly hope, *"and hope does not disappoint" (Romans 5:5).*

FOCUSING ON THE HEAVENLY PERSPECTIVE!

To wait on the Lord is to rest in the confident assurance that, regardless of the details or difficulties you face in this life, God never leaves you without a sure defence. As Moses told the panicky Israelites trapped at the Red Sea by Pharaoh's army, *"The Lord will fight for you; you need only to be still" (Exodus 14:14).* The heavenly perspective comes as you focus not on the trouble but on the Lord and His Word. When it seems God has painted you into a corner, you have an opportunity to set aside your human viewpoint and wait upon the Lord to show you His power, His purpose, and His salvation.

RENEWING YOUR STRENGTH!

Waiting on the Lord renews your strength (Isaiah 40:31). Prayer and Bible study and meditating upon God's Word are essential. To wait on the Lord you need a heart responsive to the Word of God, a focus on the things of heaven, and a patience rooted in faith.

BELIEVING THAT GOD IS GOING TO GIVE YOU THE BEST!

You should not despair when God tarries long in His response, but continue to patiently wait on Him to work on your behalf. The reason God sometimes waits a long time to deliver is to extend the goodness of the final outcome. *"Therefore the LORD waits to be gracious to you, and therefore he exalts himself to show mercy to you. For the LORD is a God of justice; blessed are all those who wait for him" (Isaiah 30:18, ESV).*

HOW LONG O LORD, HOW LONG?

"How long, O LORD? Will You forget me forever? How long will You hide Your face from me?" (Psalms 13:1 NKJV)

Never give up on something you really want. It's difficult to wait, but it's more difficult to regret. Urgh WAITING! Let's be honest, no one likes to wait! But if we really think about it, most of life is about waiting. And if you have been waiting for what seems like a life time for something/s to happen or to stop happening and you can't seem to figure out how it's going to happen, you might find yourself crying like King David, *"how long O Lord?"* How long will this trial go on for? How long will this sickness last? How long before I see a bit of light at the end of this tunnel? It's good to ask these questions, but who are you crying to? Your friends? Family? Doctor? Where does your help come from? Your help comes from the Lord, the maker of Heaven and Earth! Cry out to Him, full of hope and expectation. And He will answer.

Don't lose heart; Wait expectantly upon the Lord, Trust Him, and you will see the goodness of the Lord! King David said, *"I would have lost heart unless I had believed that I will see the goodness of the Lord in land of the living! (Psalms 27:13 NKJV)* #TrustHim

Prayer:

Father God, I know waiting is hard but at the same time I know that regretting will be even harder if I don't wait on you and the plans you have for me now. Align my heart with your heart and help me to believe that all things work together for my good at the end in Jesus name, amen.

A DESPERATE SITUATION CALLS FOR A DESPERATE PRAYER!

"O LORD of hosts, if You will indeed look on the affliction of Your maidservant andremember me, and not forget Your maidservant ... (I Samuel 1:11 NKJV)

Hardships often prepare ordinary people for an extraordinary destiny!
- C.S. Lewis

What do you do child of God when you find yourself in a situation that you know you have no control over whatsoever? No matter how much you desire to have something, there's just no way that you can make it happen yourself?

That is the kind of situation that Hannah found herself in 1 Samuel 1:1-18. The Bible says that the Lord had closed Hannah's womb so she couldn't bear children for her husband. She desired a child so much, and she would cry to the point where her husband would ask her if he wasn't good enough for her. And yet still there was no child. But I am encouraged that Hannah knew where her help would come from. Child of God you have to know where your help comes from! Your situation will mock you. People around you will mock you but just like Hannah (even though Peninnah was mocking her), you have to know who to cry out to.

Year by year Hannah would go to Shiloh to sacrifice to the Lord. She would seek the Lord even though she didn't understand why God wasn't answering her prayers right away. That is until one day.... One day she prayed a desperate prayer. She cried out desperately to the Lord, she even made a vow to the Lord, *"if you will give me a male child then I will give him back to you..."* and the priest had no choice but to come in agreement with her for whatever she had asked for and she got her miracle, baby Samuel.

Maybe you have been in a situation that feels like, or looks exactly like Hannah's story and you feel helpless. Let me encourage you by saying, seek God wholeheartedly and with all you've got! Lean not on your own understanding, give yourself wholeheartedly to God and surrender everything to Him. Let Him do only what He can do with your situation.

Don't wake up tomorrow in regret because you didn't pray today. Whatever answer He will give you, it is guaranteed to come with peace and joy! *"Go in peace, and the God of Israel grant your petition which you have asked of Him." (I Samuel 1:17 NKJV)*

Prayer:

Father God you know my heart's desires, I may not understand why I haven't got it yet but I acknowledge you in this situation and I lean not on my own understanding. Lord, I wait upon you expectantly in full faith believing that in due time I will hold my miracles in the name of Jesus. Amen.

THOUGH THE VISION TARRIES ... STILL WAIT UPON THE LORD!

"...., "No, my lord. Man of God, do not lie to your maidservant!"
(I I Kings 4:16 NKJV)

Be ready in and out of season because God can do anything anytime! - Chido Madziko

Sometimes you earnestly pray, fast and do all you know to do in order to get something you wholeheartedly desire to have, but still, not a cloud in the sky! So you pack away your dream and you put it on the shelf. Your weapons of warfare, you clean them up, pack them away and you make peace with yourself. You are not resentful, you're not bitter or angry, you just tell yourself, *"maybe I wasn't meant to have this,"* and you go on about your business. You're still going to church, you're still serving in the house of God, but somehow you have settled.

I believe this is what happened to the Shunammite Woman. As we read her story in 2 Kings 4:8-17. I believe that at one point she desired and prayed for a child, but it didn't happen as she had hoped. So she put that dream away and she went on about her business. She was good to her husband, she recognised Elisha as a man of God and built him a room in her house and served him. Eventually when Elisha asked, *"what can be done for her"*, she wasn't ready for that question. I think as children of the Most High God we should have faith in our good Father and be ready for Him to do anything, anytime. Though the vision tarries.... wait upon the Lord!

When Elisha told her that by this time next year you're going to have a baby, she said... *"No, my lord. Man of God, do not lie to your maidservant!"* *(II Kings 4:16 NKJV)* . The devil is a liar! This woman recognised Elisha as the man of God, now that same man of God is telling her that she shall have a child, and she doesn't believe him?

God knows the secret petitions of your heart. God knows that thing you desire to have but have put aside. God can do anything anytime! Hold on to the promises of God over your life. Believe and keep on believing even when it looks as if nothing is happening! Sure enough the Shunammite Woman the following year she held her baby boy in her arms.

Child of God, wait upon the Lord; keep praying; keep asking, keep knocking, keep on searching, and it shall be given to you and your joy will be full.

Prayer:

Father God, I believe that you're the God of all flesh and there's nothing too hard for you. I take my dreams off the shelf, I dust them off ready for you to do anything anytime. In Jesus mighty name, amen.

WHAT DO YOU HAVE IN YOUR HOUSE?

"So Elisha said to her, "What shall I do for you? Tell me, what do you have in the house?" And she said, "Your maidservant has nothing in the house but a jar of oil." (II Kings 4:2 NKJV)

Most of the time the very thing that we think is insignificant is the very thing that qualifies for a miracle! - Chido Madziko.

God's ways and His thoughts are higher than ours! The way that He will use to deliver us from our circumstances is totally different from our own thinking. As we read about this certain widow's story in 2 Kings 4:1-7; there are several things she did in order to get her miracle:

01. She acknowledged her problem. Don't be in denial of your problem, know that problem very well. Study that problem and know it inside and out.

02. She cried out to the man of God Elisha. She knew who would help her. Know who to cry out to for help, don't cry out to just anybody.

03. When Elisha asked her, *"What shall I do for you? Tell me, what do you have in the house?"* She was able to recognise what she had, even though she started her response by saying, *"I have nothing, but,"* but a *"but"* followed. What do you have in your house? Surely if you look with eyes of gratitude you will be able to see what God has given you to sustain you all along. He can take that and multiply it. Even though she didn't think much of that oil, but that's the very thing God used to perform a miracle.

04. She obeyed the man of God; to go and borrow empty vessels even though it didn't make sense to her. She had a creditor on her back

already so going to borrow again wouldn't make sense. But she obeyed anyway. Even when she started pouring that oil, it didn't make sense at all, but she stepped out in faith. And all the jars were filled.

The miracle or the answer to your prayers is not in the miracle itself but it's in the doing of what you have been told to do. Wait on the Lord, obey His instructions and feed on His faithfulness.

Prayer:

Father God, you're the God of multiplication, I thank you that you can take the little that I have and turn it into abundance. I surrender that which is my hands to you. Have your way Lord. I believe I receive abundance in return in Jesus mighty name, amen.

IT'S IN THE WAITING THAT YOUR FAITH IS TESTED!

"Is anything too hard for the LORD? At the appointed time I will return to you, according to the time of life, and Sarah shall have a son." (Genesis 18:14 NKJV)

"Father Abraham has many sons, many sons has Father Abraham, I am one of them and so are you so let's all praise the Lord!" If you grew up in church I am sure you will be familiar with the song. It sounds great, doesn't it?

Abraham is referred to as our father of faith. As we read his story in Genesis 18, God himself visited Abraham at his home. God Himself told Abraham, *"I will certainly return to you according to the time of life, and behold, Sarah your wife shall have a son." (Genesis 18:10 NKJV)*

Abraham believed what God told him even though in the physical it was impossible. He and his wife Sarah were well past child bearing age and on top of that Sarah was barren. But even though he believed God, he still had to wait on the Lord. Great faith doesn't mean the miraculous will happen instantly! It's in the waiting that our faith is tested.

Like Your father Abraham, you may be a person of great and unshakable faith. But being full of faith doesn't mean what you're believing for will take place right away. You still have to wait on the Lord because the promise is for an appointed time. And even though you believe what God has promised you, the temperature in the waiting room is often uncomfortable. You have to be careful that you don't start entertaining, *"what ifs,"* & *"maybes."* God doesn't need your help; His thoughts, ways and timetable are higher than yours. Eventually Abraham bore his promised child Isaac, but in the 25 years of waiting he also bore Ishmael. Be careful what you do and birth in your waiting time because an Ishmael is not easy to maintain. Wait for God's due time and you will birth miracles that will last for generations to come.

Prayer:

Father God you know I desire to have....... I ask for this in the name of Jesus. Lord, by the power of your Holy Spirit help me to wait on you. Help me to wait for your due date. Help me to be strong and steady trusting you at all times. In Jesus name, amen.

BY HIS SPIRIT YOU WILL RISE FROM THE ASHES OF DEFEAT!

"I press toward the goal for the prize of the upward call of God in Christ Jesus." (Philippians 3:14 NKJV)

Rise above the storm and you will find the sunshine!

LIFE - It has happened to all of us, hasn't it? We've all had to face tough times, and unimaginable things have happened to all of us. But even though we all go through challenges, no one can truly understand your situation but you. Yes family and friends can sympathise and you could have great encouragement around you but at the end of the day YOU have to decide and YOU have to get up and do something if you want your situation to change. Are you waiting on God to change your situation or are you just waiting for whatever happens to happen?

Are you going to continue to sit in your pit of despair and cry over what has happened? A pit of despair can be very comfortable if you allow it but it takes you nowhere, it will only pull you down deeper and deeper! RISE! *"Forget those things that lie behind and press on towards a new goal."* It's not easy, but a made up mind is a powerful thing! Give the eye of your mind a new goal, a new target and press on towards that.

"Look unto Jesus, the author and finisher of our faith, who for the joy that was set before Him endured the cross, despising the shame, and has sat down at the right hand of the throne of God." (Hebrews 12:2 NKJV) You too will come out on the other end victorious. #TrustHim

Prayer:

Father God, I decide today to get out of the pit. What happened happened but I refuse to be in despair! I believe you are causing all things to workout for my good for I love you and have been called according to your purpose in Jesus name, amen.

PRAY!

"Hear my cry, O God; Attend to my prayer. From the end of the earth I will cry to You, When my heart is overwhelmed; Lead me to the rock that is higher than I. For You have been a shelter for me, A strong tower from the enemy. I will abide in Your tabernacle forever; I will trust in the shelter of Your wings. Selah" (Psalms 61:1-4 NKJV)

The prayer of a righteous person is powerful and effective! Be a prayer warrior! Your battles must be won in the spiritual realm first, then in the physical!

As Sovereign as God is, He will not answer a prayer that you did not pray! Prayer is simply talking to God about anything, anytime and anywhere. It is not complicated! If you don't know how to pray, I encourage you to go and read some of the prayerful psalms in the Bible. They will give you a good starting point. I love the relationship King David had with God; He told God everything! And I mean everything; whether he was in a valley hiding from his enemies or he was on a mountain top celebrating his victories, he would always talk to God.

Jesus, the Son of the living God, prayed - all the time! He would go to solitary places and pray. He encouraged His disciples to pray. He even prayed for you! John dedicated a whole chapter to Jesus's prayer; in chapter 17 Jesus prayed for Himself, He prayed for His disciples, and he prayed for you. When He was about to face the cross, He prayed, *"saying, "Father, if it is Your will, take this cup away from Me; nevertheless not My will, but Yours, be done." (Luke 22:42 NKJV.)* He prayed for Peter, *"Simon! Indeed, Satan has asked for you, that he may sift you as wheat. But I have prayed for you," (Luke 22:31-32 NKJV.)*

Pray for your spirit to be strong in the Lord and in the power of His might! Pray for your spouse - if you're not yet married pray for your future spouse! Pray for your children - if you don't have kids yet, pray for your future children! Pray for your family! Pray for your health! Pray for your job! Pray for your future! Pray for your city! Pray for your country! Pray for everything! PRAY!

DRAW STRENGTH FROM GOD THROUGH PRAYER!

"In the day when I cried out, You answered me, And made me bold with strength in my soul." (Psalms 138:3 NKJV)

Prayer is simply having a conversation with God. I love the Psalms because as we read them we come to understand why God said about David, *"a man after my own heart!"* David shows us what it's like to have a one to one conversation with God; David didn't talk about God, but he talked with God. I am encouraging you today to have a personal relationship with God; talk with Him on a one to one level, tell Him anything and everything. That's what Prayer is; simply talking with God.

Let God be your first point of contact, let Him be the first person you talk to about any situation at any given time. God doesn't look at the outward appearance but He looks at the heart.

He already knows what's inside your heart; your dreams, your vision, your heartbreaks, he knows everything. And that's why He says, *"And you will seek Me and find Me, when you search for Me with all your heart."* *(Jeremiah 29:13 NKJV).* David says things like, "I waited patiently for the Lord, He inclined to me and heard my cry." He is actually testifying that God heard him and listened to him when he cried to Him. Child of God, God will hear you, He knows your voice, He knows your deepest heart's desires, talk to Him. And you too will testify to the glory of God.

Prayer:

Father God, I desire for You to call me a woman or man after your Own heart! Help me by the Spirit of Your Son in me crying, *"ABBA Father,"* to talk with you and even cry to you about anything and everything In Jesus name, amen.

PUSH THROUGH FEAR AND ADVERSITY!

"Wait on the LORD; Be of good courage, And He shall strengthen your heart; Wait, I say, on the LORD!" (Psalms 27:14 NKJV)

Fear is a reaction. Courage is a decision ...

The Bible says, *"above all else guard your heart with all diligence for everything you do flows from it." (Proverbs 4:23).* In Psalm 27:14, David is telling us to be of good courage, and God will strengthen our hearts. As you wait on the Lord, waiting is not just sitting down doing nothing, but your attitude while you're waiting. While you're waiting, you will face all sorts of challenges. Your faith will be tested-Remember the enemy is also doing all that he can to make sure that you fail.

When your faith is being challenged that's when you will need to be of good courage. To be of good courage is to have the quality of mind or spirit that enables a person to face difficulty, danger, pain, etc., without fear; bravery - Strength in the face of pain or grief. And only the Spirit of God can enable you to do that. And this is the Word of the Lord to you: *Not by might nor by power, but by My Spirit,' Says the LORD of hosts." (Zechariah 4:6 NKJV)*

Courage is trusting God enough to do what He is calling you to do in the midst of adversity. Trust God, wait upon Him and He will never allow shame to come upon you.

Pray:

Father God, help me by the power of Your Holy Spirit to be strong and courageous as I wait on you. I believe that you will never allow shame to come into my life in Jesus name I pray, amen.

BELIEVE!

"Therefore I say to you, whatever things you ask when you pray, believe that you receive them, and you will have them." (Mark 11:24 NKJV)

Prayer is the key to heaven, but faith unlocks the door. This is a Bible verse that you just have to take as it is; you swallow it, you keep on praying and believe that you will have what you're asking for in prayer! Because if you try to understand how it works it will knock you upside down! Have faith in God! Your faith has to override your carnal mind! You're walking by faith and not by sight! You're only looking at Jesus, the author and finisher of your faith. Faith is the substance of things hoped for, the evidence of things not seen (Hebrews 11:1) *"Without faith it is impossible to please Him, for he who comes to God must believe that He is, and that He is a rewarder of those who diligently seek Him." (Hebrews 11:6 NKJV)*

Feed on the word of God! Faith comes by hearing and hearing by the word of God. Jesus said, if you abide in Me and My words abide in you, you will ask what you desire and it shall be done for you. *"Now this is the confidence that we have in Him, that if we ask anything according to His will, He hears us. And if we know that He hears us, whatever we ask, we know that we have the petitions that we have asked of Him." (I John 5:14-15 NKJV)*

You will only know the will of God when you know who God is. And you will only know who God is when you read His word. Man shall not live by bread alone but by every word that proceeds from the mouth of God. By faith, claim the answer to your request. If you know you are abiding in Christ and are controlled by the Holy Spirit and are praying according to the Word and will of God, you can expect God to answer your prayer. So be prepared to receive the answer. Imagine right now that you are receiving the answer to your request, and begin to thank God for it.

Prayer:

Father God, I pray in Jesus name, the author and finisher of my faith and I let my requests be made known to you. I ask in accordance to your will. In full faith I believe that I receive all that I have asked for in this prayer. Thank you Lord, amen.

HOLD ONTO YOUR DREAMS!

"And they said to him, *"We each have had a dream, and there is no interpreter of it."* So Joseph said to them, *"Do not interpretations belong to God? Tell them to me, please." (Genesis 40:8 NKJV).*

You have to hold onto your dreams and never give up. You may not accomplish what you want at a certain age. That doesn't mean it will not happen. Keep on trying. - JOYCE WILLIAMS

Sometimes God shows us a glimpse of our future, but the route that He uses to get us there is totally different from the one we imagine. Often times it will look as if we're lost & we're going in the wrong direction. And we start to wonder; *"Am I headed in the right direction?"* *"God are you even here?"* God showed Joseph his future and He showed it to him in the form of dreams that needed to be interpreted. *(Genesis 37).* Joseph had an idea of what his dreams meant, his father and his brothers knew what they meant, but as to how it was going to come about I am sure all of them had no idea. Because in an attempt to kill his dreams, his brothers sold him to foreigners and Joseph was taken to Egypt not knowing that they were actually ushering him into the right place for his dreams to come true. Later on he was accused of something that he didn't do and he was put in a prison, and it's when he was in the prison that his purpose manifested.

Child of God, the interpretation of your dreams belong God! Don't allow other people or even yourself to interpret your dreams because God's ways are higher than yours and His thoughts are higher than yours. To Him a day is like a thousand and a thousand is like a day. Sometimes it may look as if God has forgotten all about you, but just like the Bible says, *"But the LORD was with Joseph and showed him mercy, and He gave him favor in the sight of the keeper of the prison." (Genesis 39:21 NKJV).* The Lord is with you; He never leaves you not forsake you, He will show you His favour, mercy and grace. And when it is time to bring you out, He will do it in style and honour! Be still and know that He is God!

God knows you best and He's never wrong or late. Trust Him & lean not on your own understanding, He is directing your steps. Even if it feels like you are in a dungeon, as long as you have your full faith in God and you believe that He is ordering your steps, you're there for a reason and the purpose He has for you will be revealed to you. Joseph came out on the other end the second highest man in Egypt and his brothers had to come bowing down to him just as he had seen in his dreams. Child of God as long as you trust God, He will not allow shame to come upon you.

Prayer:

Father God, you're the giver and the interpreter of my dreams. I pray Lord and ask in Jesus name that I stay in the lane that which you have for me to reach the fulfilment of my dreams. Help me and strengthen me by the power of your Holy Spirit. Amen.

Chapter Thirteen

A NET BREAKING BREAKTHROUGH

"But Simon answered and said to Him, "Master, we have toiled all night and caught nothing; nevertheless at Your word I will let down the net." (Luke 5:5 NKJV).

We can all relate to Simon's response can't we? Especially the first part of his response to Jesus. There are situations and circumstances you have been praying and seeking the Lord for a while now that even if Jesus was to come to you personally and tell you to *"launch into the deep for a catch,"* your first response will be, "Lord, I have been praying about this situation for a long time." "I have been confessing your word over my child for a while now." "I have been fasting every week for some time now but the situation hasn't been changing."

But all you need is one word from the Lord and your story will change instantly. You have to be ready to listen when God speaks to you. He is the God of all flesh and there's nothing too hard for Him. He can speak to you using anyone or anything. You have to have a *"nevertheless,"* ready when God gives you instructions on how to do certain things. When He tells you to pray in a specific way or even move to a different city. You have been doing things your way for some time now and nothing has been changing so why won't you listen when God tells you to do something different? Obedience is better than sacrifice!

Sure enough Simon listened and obeyed Jesus *"And when they had done this, they caught a great number of fish, and their net was breaking." (Luke 5:6 NKJV).* Wouldn't you want to have a net breaking breakthrough, simply because you obeyed God? To have your net start breaking from all the answers to your prayers because God is able to do exceedingly, abundantly, above all that you can ask or think! (Ephesians 3:20).

Obey God and you will have more than enough to be a blessing to others too.

Prayer:

Father God, I pray and I thank you that you're forever talking. I ask in the name of Jesus that you help me listen to your words of wisdom and not only listen but to obey you. I wait upon you Lord expectantly. Amen.

WATCH YOUR THOUGHTS!

"Let the words of my mouth and the meditation of my heart Be acceptable in Your sight, O LORD, my strength and my Redeemer." (Psalms 19:14 NKJV)

Be the coach of your own soul!

The best sermon you will ever hear is the one you preach to yourself putting all your hope in God and not yourself! Because if you preach to yourself from yourself it will always lead to scarcity, it will lead to anxiety, fears and worries! We are human beings! Do you know what that means? It means we're impatient, short sighted, we grumble, we complain, basically we are a mess. That's why child of God you need to look to Jesus, the author and finisher of your faith. You cannot look and rely on yourself. Put your faith in God, He is your source and His grace is sufficient. Greater is He who is in you than he that is in the world. The love of God has been shed abroad in your heart. Yield your heart and your spirit to Jesus who is your hope. *"Now hope does not disappoint, because the love of God has been poured out in our hearts by the Holy Spirit who was given to us." (Romans 5:5 NKJV)*

God has promised you great things, but as you wait for those promises to come to pass, your own heart may deceive you! Beware of the self-critical voice that will try to defeat you before you even start! It will try to rob you of any credit for anything that you do, and makes you afraid of trying anything because you fear it's not going to work out! Be strong in the Lord and in the power of His might.

Prayer:

Father God, I pray in Jesus name, you're the anchor of my soul! Help me to put my hope in you and you alone. I will not allow my heart to condemn me. I look to you Lord, the source of life. I receive the life Jesus came to give me.

Amen.

RECEIVE THE PEACE OF GOD!

"Peace I leave with you, My peace I give to you; not as the world gives do I give to you. Let not your heart be troubled, neither let it be afraid." (John 14:27 NKJV)

Worrying does not take tomorrow's trouble; it takes away today's peace.

You were never made to worry! Jesus said, *"Do not worry about tomorrow, for tomorrow will worry about its own things."* He even goes on to say worrying doesn't change one thing. Worrying is like sitting on a rocking chair, you're moving but you're not going anywhere! I know you have needs, wants and desires you want to see fulfilled in your life. And sometimes you can't even see how it's going to happen, so you worry. In other words, you're fearful that it's not going to happen! I know that worrying is something that grows as you grow because when you were little you didn't worry. So me telling you *"not to worry,"* you are probably thinking, *"easier said than done,"* right? Yes, it's hard if you try to do it on your own. That's why *"as you wait ..."* you need to put your trust in God. As you wait on the Lord, you give God your worries and He gives you His peace that surpasses all understanding. God will put your heart at ease. He wants you to guard your heart with all diligence! Better yet, let the peace of God guard your heart & mind. To guard is to *"watch over in order to protect or control."*

Wouldn't you want God's peace to protect and control your heart and mind? Do not be anxious about anything but in everything let your requests be made known to God, and the peace of God which surpasses all understanding, will guard your heart & mind! (Philippians 4:6-7) Jesus said, *"Peace I leave with you, My peace I give to you; not as the world gives do I give to you. Let not your heart be troubled, neither let it be afraid." (John 14:27 NKJV)* #TrustHim

Prayer:

Father God, today I receive your peace that surpasses all understanding. I refuse to worry anymore and I cast my burdens unto Jesus for He cares for me. As I wait Lord for my needs, wants & desires to be fulfilled I put my full faith in you and believe that you will provide in Jesus name, amen.

REALISE THAT YOUR LIFE HAS DIFFERENT SEASONS

"To everything there is a season, A time for every purpose under heaven:"
(Ecclesiastes 3:1 NKJV)

Seed - Time - Harvest!

Our seasons of life differ, don't compare your seasons to someone else's! We go through different seasons in life and we are ok as long as we are in the spring and summer seasons of our life; I mean everything is new, rosy, warm and fuzzy, right? Who wouldn't want that! But oh no, as soon as we enter the autumn and winter seasons of our life where everything is dark and gloomy we become unsettled! Let's be honest no one wants dark and gloomy, but I believe that's when God does the most important work in you! That's when He strengthens you! That's when you grow your roots! That's when He brings out the best that is in you! I know sometimes when you're in a dark place you think that you've been buried, but child, you're not buried, but you have actually been planted! Wait until you start sprouting and blossoming!

A seed is full of all the potential to become a full grown plant that will yield a harvest, but if it's not planted in the right ground and protected it comes to nothing. So in order for you to come out shining & blossoming on the other side of your winter days, God has to protect that precious seed He has put inside of you. For your life to become beautiful in its time God has to hide you in a secret place for a season. He makes sure you're protected, you're watered and you have enough sunlight.

Your life is hid with Christ in God! Abide in Christ Jesus, your breakthrough is in the breaking. As you abide in Christ, He takes you, breaks you, and mould you into a beautiful and fruitful plant. Jesus said, *"I am the vine and you are the branch and without me you cannot do anything!" (John 15:5)*

Prayer:

Father God, I surrender myself to abide in Christ as He is the vine and I am the branch. I want to bear much fruit. Help me to stay grounded Lord in Jesus name, amen.

ALL THINGS WORK TOGETHER FOR YOU

"And we know that all things work together for good to those who love God, to those who are the called according to His purpose." (Romans 8:28 NKJV)

"You shall love the LORD your God with all your heart, with all your soul, and with all your strength." (Deuteronomy 6:5 NKJV)

The Lord our God is one and besides Him there is no other! And when you love God with all your heart, and with all your soul, and with all your strength that means you have a personal relationship with Him. That means you know Him to come through for you in every situation and circumstance. That's why Apostle Paul was able to say with confidence, *"and we know that all things work together for good "to those who love God ..."* because He had a personal relationship with God, and He had seen Him come through for him and those who love Him before.

I really encourage you to seek the Lord in every situation and circumstance; He is a rewarder of those who diligently seek Him. Call upon Him and He will show you great and mighty things you do not know! The more you call upon Him, the more He shows you His love, power, and purpose. He will deliver you from your enemies. He is your rock, defence, salvation, shield, strength, etc.

David said, *"I will love You, O LORD, my strength. The LORD is my rock and my fortress and my deliverer; My God, my strength, in whom I will trust; My shield and the horn of my salvation, my stronghold. I will call upon the LORD, who is worthy to be praised; So shall I be saved from my enemies." (Psalms 18:1-3 NKJV)*. David believed that no matter what He goes through all things will work out for his good to him because he was a man after God's heart. Be a person who is after God's heart.

As you wait on the Lord believe that God has a purpose for you that is far greater than you can imagine. Don't let the struggle you are currently going through keep you from the blessings that God has for you. When you go through the fire and the water believe that God is with you all the way and He is bringing you out on the other side victorious and glorious.

In Jeremiah 29:11 He says, *"For I know the plans I have for you,"* declares the Lord, *"plans to prosper you and not to harm you, plans to give you hope and a future."*

Prayer:

Father God, I will love you Lord my strength, shield and rock. You are my all in all. Give me a heart that is after you Lord, and I believe that as I wait on You, all things are working together for good to me in every situation and circumstance in Jesus name. Amen.

ALLOW YOURSELF TO BE QUIET BEFORE GOD!

"A time to tear, And a time to sew; A time to keep silence, And a time to speak;" (Ecclesiastes 3:7 NKJV)

A quiet mind is able to hear intuition over fear! TRAIN YOUR MIND TO BE STILL! As long as you're breathing your mind can never be still! Your mind is always in search of answers, solutions and reasons why somethings are happening or not happening. God has given you a brilliant tool that you can use to change your life - your mind is brilliant, but your spirit has to rule over your mind! Romans 12:2 says, *"And do not be conformed to this world, but be transformed by the renewing of your mind, that you may prove what is that good and acceptable and perfect will of God." (Romans 12:2 NKJV)*

Child of God, God has a perfect plan and a perfect will for your life. Sometimes you don't need to know everything that God is doing in you and through you right away; be still and know that God knows what He is doing. Trust Him! Trusting God means you have a firm belief in the reliability, truth, or ability of the Almighty God. You believe that your steps are ordered by the LORD, and that He delights in your way. Though you fall, you shall not be utterly cast down; For the LORD upholds you with His hand. You have been young, and now you're old; Yet you have not seen the righteous forsaken, Nor his descendants begging bread. (Psalms 37:23-25 NKJV). He has you in the palm of His hands.

It is the glory of God to conceal a matter... (Proverbs 25:2). Sometimes God doesn't reveal somethings to you straight away because you're not ready to handle them therefore He'll be protect you from making mistakes. You would rather wait on the Lord than get yourself more messed up because sometimes in search of answers, solutions and reasons why, you will get yourself in even more trouble than you were in before! God's timing is the best timing!

Prayer:

Father God, I pray in Jesus name, help me by the power of your Holy Spirit to set my eyes on things above, not on the earth. Help me trust you completely that I do not worry, but believe that you're ordering my steps into the perfect will you have for me. Thank you Lord, I believe that it is done! Amen

WRITE THE VISION DOWN!

"For the vision is yet for an appointed time; But at the end it will speak, and it will not lie. Though it tarries, wait for it; Because it will surely come, It will not tarry." (Habakkuk 2:3 NKJV)

Vision is a picture of the future that produces passion!

We don't live our lives for today but for tomorrow or rather for the future. You go to school for your future. You go to work for your future. You get married and have children for your future. God did not just create you to be born and sit here on Earth and do nothing! *"From beginning "... the LORD God took the man and put him in the Garden of Eden to tend and keep it. (Genesis 2:15 NKJV)*

You have God given gifts, talents, and desires. Some gifts you can quickly identify because they come easy to you from when you were a child. Some will come by inspiration, and yet some you just feel a tug at your heart to do something. God puts these gifts, talents, and desires in your heart and they become your vision. And the first step to bringing your vision to life is to write these things down. Pray about them, believe that with God's help you can do it! Put your faith into action and bring them to reality.

In every step of the way inquire of the Lord, wait upon Him, listen to His instructions, be very fervent is prayer! *"For the vision is yet for an appointed time; But at the end it will speak, and it will not lie. Though it tarries, wait for it; Because it will surely come, It will not tarry." (Habakkuk 2:3 NKJV)*

Prayer:

Father God, here is my vision. I wait upon you Lord, lead me and guide me in the way that I should go in order to bring my vision to pass. I bless it, I sanctify it and I believe that it shall bring you glory in Jesus name, amen.

YOU ARE OF GREAT VALUE!

"I will praise You, for I am fearfully and wonderfully made; Marvelous are Your works, And that my soul knows very well." (Psalms 139:14 NKJV)

You are valuable because you exist, not because of what you do or what you have done, but simply because you're! – Max Lucado

It's unfortunate that we are now living in an age where everyone is identified by what they do, and what they have. Being just you doesn't seem to count anymore! And as a result, we don't know who we really are anymore! Which is really sad, because when you're born you physically appear in this world holding nothing but the world rejoices! But as you grow older the world changes its view about you.

I am here to encourage you and tell you that your worth is found in God and God alone. The only thing that matters and that will stand is what God says about you! If you have been feeling like you're worth nothing because there are some things you have been waiting to happen and they haven't happened yet, child of God, you're blessed and highly favoured. The world is distorted, it will always talk and have an opinion. Focus on who you are and not on what you have or don't have!

You are valuable, you are needed and without your puzzle piece your family, church, even the world wouldn't be complete. So don't get caught up in the pressure to change and conform because you will begin to lose your identity in the process. We were all designed to be special and unique; God has given us all different skills, passions and characteristics. You were not created to fit in, you were created by God to be you and only you. And as you wait on God, *"Do not fear, little flock,*

for it is your Father's good pleasure to give you the kingdom."
(Luke 12:32 NKJV)

Prayer:

Father God, thank you that I am fearfully and wonderfully made, created in your image. Nothing missing and nothing broken! Thank you Lord that my life is hid with Christ in you Jehovah! Amen.

BELIEVING GOD FOR BOAZ!

"Blessed is she who believed, for there will be a fulfillment of those things which were told her from the Lord." (Luke 1:45 NKJV)

DELAY IS NOT DENIAL AND WAITING IS NOT PUNISHMENT BUT PREPARATION!

"GOD WHERE IS MY BOAZ?" If you're over 28 and you are not married yet and if at one point you thought you would be married at the age of 25 and it hasn't happened yet, I can bet you have uttered that question once or twice. You see, marriage was designed by the Almighty God Himself, your creator and I believe that God plants that seed of desiring a husband in all of us, (unless you're one of the special people God has set aside to dedicate themselves to the work of the Lord). But if not, you have that desire inside of you to have a God fearing husband, have beautiful children and become a family.

But it hasn't happened yet! And now you feel like you have been waiting for what seems like eternity. That Bible verse that says, *"It's not good for man to be alone"* begins to make real sense. It's not like you don't want Boaz, you do. With all your heart you genuinely desire to have someone to love you and love back, someone who will have your back and share everything with... and you look at other married couples and you're like, I wish...

My sister do not lose heart! *BELIEVE!* With God all things are possible. Believe that the same God who planted that desire in you is the same God who will bring it to fruition. Don't look down upon yourself, you deserve the very best God has to give you. You're beautiful and you're worth it. Tell yourself and believe it, *"delay is not denial!"* *"Waiting isn't punishment, its preparation!"* You have to preach to yourself. You have to be a prayerful woman. Dress nice! Go to places. Be confident! Be prepared! God will not put you to shame! And when God sends you the man you're called to be with ... you will know. This man will not speak to your flesh but to your spirit. You will experience something in him that you have never experienced before. He will love you in ways that other man didn't. Wait! It will be so worth it when you meet him.

Prayer:

Father God, you know what's best for me. Lord, I want the best that you have for me-the best Boaz, the best love, the best connection. Lord, help me not to miss when my Boaz shows up. I wait upon you Lord, expectantly, for your glory in Jesus name, amen.

BELIEVING GOD FOR HEALING!

"Jesus said to him, "If you can believe, all things are possible to him who believes." (Mark 9:23 NKJV)

"I am the Lord who heals you" (Exodus 15:26) It is God's will for you to be healed! You have to believe that with all your being! Paul prayed, *"Beloved, I pray that you may prosper in all things and be in health, just as your soul prospers." (III John 1:2 NKJV)*

If you have been sick or a loved one has been ill for a while and you haven't received any healing yet, don't lose hope. Have faith in God. And how do you have faith or grow your faith in God? Faith comes by hearing and hearing by the word of God. (Romans 10:17). And where do you find the word of God! In the Bible. You have to look up scriptures on healing.

The Bible is full of healing testimonies. You have to meditate on the Word of God, utter it over and over again. You have to believe what you're reading, you're not reading just an ordinary story book. The word of God is living and powerful, it is healing to your bones. God sends His Word to heal you. Jesus said, "the words that I speak to you, they are life." And that's exactly what God wants to do - to release life into your body.

Almost everyone in the Bible that Jesus healed, He would say, *"go in peace, your faith has made you whole."* Or *"may it be done according to your faith."* *"Now faith is the substance of things hoped for, the evidence of things not seen." (Hebrews 11:1 NKJV).* *"Believe that God can and will heal you. Be very prayerful; the effective, fervent prayer of a righteous man avails much." (James 5:16 NKJV).*

Sickness is a curse, and you're a blessed child of God. Sickness should not be part of you. Pray and bind every generational sicknesses, bind negativity words that might have been released over your life in the name of Jesus, the name that is above every other name. God said, I am the Lord who heals you. Call unto Him for healing, talk to Him about your situation in prayer. He already knows, He is waiting for you.

Prayer:

Father God, you're the God of all flesh and there is nothing too hard for you. I believe that you can heal me, I believe that I receive healing in my body where healing is needed now. I receive strength, remedy and restoration in my body in the name of Jesus. Thank you Lord.

BELIEVING GOD FOR A JOB!

"Ask, and it will be given to you; seek, and you will find; knock, and it will be opened to you." (Matthew 7:7 NKJV)

The more you believe and trust God, the more limitless possibilities become for your family, your career - for your life! Unemployment is one of the toughest experiences a person can go through in their life. And truth be told sometimes it can lead to depression and sickness. The struggle is real and frustrating! I mean, It's not like you're lazy, or you don't want to work, no! You're a hard worker and you genuinely need a job, but it isn't happening yet. No job means no money, and you need money to keep a roof over your head and food on the table. *"Money answers everything,"* the Bible says.

If you're looking for a job right now I encourage you to trust God completely! I mean your faith has to be 100% on God to grant you favour to get picked for the job/s you're applying for. Ask God to surround you and your job applications with unmerited favour. Don't lose heart, don't despair. Stand on the Word of God nonstop; look up scriptures that relate to jobs and employment. Confess the word of God out loud over your situation again and again, even if it looks as if nothing is happening. Personalise scripture over your situation. In the spiritual realm things are changing; first of all you must win in the spiritual realm then you will win in the physical.

- . HAVE FAITH IN GOD
- . BE VERY PRAYERFUL
- . STAND ON THE WORD OF GOD
- . CONFESS THE WORD OF GOD

. PERSONALISE THE WORD

May the beauty of the Lord our God be upon you and establish the work of your hands, yes establish the work of your hands. (Psalm 90:17)

Trust in the Lord with all your heart and lean not on your own understanding. (Proverbs 3:5)

Ask and it will be given to you; seek and you will find; knock and the door will be opened to you. (Matthew 7:7)

And we know that in all things God works for the good of those who love him, who have been called according to his purpose. (Romans 8:28)

Prayer:

Father God, I call upon you Jehovah Jireh, the Lord will provide, Your Word says, you surround me with favour as a shield. Lord, I ask for that favour to manifest now in my job applications, grant me success to get a good paying job. You supply all of my need Lord, I believe that I receive in Jesus name. Amen.

BELIEVING GOD FOR MARRIAGE RESTORATION!

"Again He said to me, "Prophesy to these bones, and say to them, 'O dry bones, hear the word of the LORD! Thus says the Lord GOD to these bones: "Surely I will cause breath to enter into you, and you shall live." (Ezekiel 37:4-5 NKJV)

God is a God of restoration. When we place the broken pieces of our lives in His hands, He restores them to a beauty that outshines the former. I remember watching this movie called War Room, and Ms Clara, (an elderly lady who was advising this young woman named Elizabeth who was having problems in her marriage) said, *"you need to fight the real enemy of your marriage, which is the devil. The enemy comes to steal, kill, & destroy! He is stealing your joy, killing your faith, & trying to destroy your marriage!"* She continued, *"You have to go into your war room and fight on your knees in prayer to God. Lift up the sword of the Spirit which is the Word of God and fight for your husband, marriage, children, joy."*

Elizabeth started to go into her war room frequently. She would shut the door behind her, and begin to pray for her husband and their marriage. She got hold of James 4:7, which says,*"Therefore submit to God. Resist the devil and he will flee from you." (James 4:7 NKJV).*

She recited this verse out loud over and over again and as she kept on reciting it the eyes of her understanding were opening wider and wider and finally she understood what she was supposed to do! She came out of her war room and she said, *"devil I know you can hear me! I kick you out of this house, you don't belong here, you can't have my husband, my marriage, my children and you certainly can't have my joy, because my joy does not come from my job, or even my husband, but my joy comes from Jesus!"* Child of God, marriage breakdown is one of the hardest experiences one could go through in life. Marriage, once broken will take the grace of God to bring it to restoration. This is a fight you cannot fight alone! If you fight alone you will fail because it's not just you in it; there's you, your spouse, and the devil. You need a fourth man in this fire; His name is Jesus, and your victory will be certain. Ms Clara said to Elizabeth, *"Victory begins at the point of surrendering to Jesus. There isn't enough room for you and God on the throne of your heart, it's either you or Him, you need to step down!"*

Sometimes the devil blinds us so bad that even if we try our hardest, we can't even see where or when it all began to go wrong, but God knows. Ask God to open your eyes to see beyond the physical, marriage is a spiritual battle! And most of the times it's not the big things that destroy us, but it is the little foxes that spoil the vine. Trust God completely, surrender all to Him, and He will give you beauty for ashes.

Prayer:

Father God, I believe that you're the God of restoration. Lord I ask you in the name of Jesus, restore my marriage. I repent of my sins, I acknowledge my wrong doing, correct me Lord. Unite me and my spouse together in Christ Jesus. We submit to you, we resist the devil and we believe that he is fleeing right now! In Jesus name, amen.

PERSONAL TESTIMONY!

"But Simon answered and said to Him, "Master, we have toiled all night and caught nothing; nevertheless at Your word I will let down the net." (Luke 5:5 NKJV)

The Holy Ghost speaks with a voice that you feel more than you hear... While we speak of listening to the whisperings of the Spirit, most often one describes a spiritual prompting by saying, *"I had a feeling..."*

I remember 12 years ago when I received the news that my dad had become unwell. I was in the United Kingdom at that time and I couldn't go back home to Zimbabwe to see him. My dad had received what was the saddest news of his life. (The doctors said, take him home there's nothing that we can do for him anymore.) More to the point, he was told that he was dying. I remember receiving that same sad news and I became tormented in my mind and emotions.

That time in Zimbabwe cell phone networks were not wide spread like they are now, and to make matters worse my parents' home was in the rural areas. That meant having cell phone reception there, was a miracle. Our next door neighbour had a cell phone, I picked up my phone in one hand and a calling card in another and I tried to ring that number from Monday to Friday without getting through. I was hopeless and anxious, *"what is my dad thinking?" "Is he upset with me because I wasn't able to talk to him let alone see him?"* I prayed like I had never prayed before.

That time my relationship with God was not as personal as it is now. I would only pray when something was really wrong. So I tried to call that number from Monday to Friday without getting through. All you could hear on the other side was dead silence. On Saturday I woke up as usual and I set on my bed and dialled that number that I now knew so well by heart, but still there was only dead silence. I tried a couple of times more, but still nothing. I got so frustrated that I threw the phone and the calling card on the bed not knowing what to do anymore.

Right then... I heard this still small voice coming from within me say, *"try one more time." "WHAT!"* I answered that voice, *"what's the point in trying one more time? I have been ringing this number for the whole week every day but it hasn't been working. What difference is it going to make now?"* The still small voice said again, *"try one more time."* I said ok I will dial the number just to prove you wrong. I rang the number again and after a few seconds I almost jumped off the bed because I could hear a ringing tone coming from the other end of the line. I couldn't believe it, the phone was actually ringing!

My older sister picked up the phone, she was crying and I knew straight away "what had happened", but my mind went straight into denial mode. My sister couldn't bring herself to tell me so she passed the phone to my auntie and my auntie broke the news to me that my dad had passed away the previous night. I talked and cried with my mum and other relatives. I called back again and we were able to make funeral arrangements. I was able to buy my dad a coffin and I bought food for people to eat at the funeral, because that time things were really hard in Zimbabwe.

And after the funeral I heard God whispering to me, *"Chido, that line opening, that still small voice telling you to try one more time, I did that for you. I gave you an opportunity to do something for your dad that no one else was able to do so that you will have peace."* Sure enough I tried to ring that number again after making the funeral arrangements but I couldn't get through, it went back to dead silence. That's when I realised that truly God was with me. And sure enough I received peace that surpasses all understanding. Yes I might not have been able to see my dad when he was ill or attend his funeral but God gave me an opportunity to honour my dad and I am forever grateful for that. If I had not listened to that still small voice to try one more time I would have missed on a golden opportunity, and I would have lived in regret my whole life. No matter what situation you find yourself in, wait upon the Lord, listen to His voice and instructions. It may not make sense at the time, but obey the voice of the Lord anyway and you won't regret it.

PRAYER FOR YOU

Father God, the creator of Heaven and Earth, the Father of our Lord and Savour Jesus Christ and the giver of the Holy Spirit. You are worthy of all our praise and adoration, you're our God and besides you there's no other. It is in Jesus name that I boldly come to the throne of grace and pray to you lifting up everyone who has been waiting on you.

Lord, your word says that the prayer of the righteous avails much and I have been made the righteousness of God in Christ Jesus. I pray that You God of our Lord Jesus Christ, the Father of glory, may give your sons and daughters the spirit of wisdom and revelation in the knowledge of You, the eyes of their understanding being enlightened; that they may know what is the hope of Your calling, what are the riches of the glory of Your inheritance in the saints, and what is the exceeding greatness of Your power toward them who believe, according to the working of Your mighty power which You worked in Christ when You raised Him from the dead and seated Him at Your right hand in the heavenly places. (Ephesians 1:17-20 NKJV)

Father, You know the desires and petitions of Your sons and Your daughters hearts. As they wait on You Lord, may they abide in Christ and may the words of Christ abide in them. May they come after you whole heartedly, seek you with all their hearts and call to you in full faith believing that you will answer and show them great and mighty things that they do not know!

You're renewing their strength; they shall mount up with wings like eagles, they shall run and not grow weary, they shall walk and not faint towards that purpose and calling you have for them. Delay is not denial! I pray that they will lean not on their own understanding, but acknowledge You in all they do and never lose heart. Thank you Lord that you've heard this prayer and answered it already.

Thank you Lord for granting them their requests. Thank you Lord that they shall testify to your glory. For Yours is the kingdom, the power and the glory! Thank You that your promises are yes and amen in Christ Jesus. Amen.

SCRIPTURE ON WAITING ON THE LORD...

"For the word of God is living and powerful, and sharper than any two-edged sword, piercing even to the division of soul and spirit, and of joints and marrow, and is a discerner of the thoughts and intents of the heart." *Hebrews 4:12 NKJV*

"So you, by the help of your God, return; Observe mercy and justice, And wait on your God continually." *Hosea 12:6 NKJV*

"Wait on the LORD; Be of good courage, And He shall strengthen your heart; Wait, I say, on the LORD!" *Psalms 27:14 NKJV*

"Rest in the LORD, and wait patiently for Him; Do not fret because of him who prospers in his way, Because of the man who brings wicked schemes to pass." *Psalms 37:7 NKJV*

"Behold, as the eyes of servants look to the hand of their masters, As the eyes of a maid to the hand of her mistress, So our eyes look to the LORD our God, Until He has mercy on us." *Psalms 123:2 NKJV*

"Lead me in Your truth and teach me, For You are the God of my salvation; On You I wait all the day." *Psalms 25:5 NKJV*

"My voice You shall hear in the morning, O LORD; In the morning I will direct it to You, And I will look up." *Psalms 5:3*

"Our soul waits for the LORD; He is our help and our shield. For our heart shall rejoice in Him, Because we have trusted in His holy name." *Psalms 33:20-21 NKJV*

"I wait for the LORD, my soul waits, And in His word I do hope." *Psalms 130:5 NKJV*

"Behold, You desire truth in the inward parts, And in the hidden part You will make me to know wisdom." *Psalms 51:6 NKJV*

"The eyes of all look expectantly to You, And You give them their food in due season. You open Your hand And satisfy the desire of every living thing." *Psalms 145:15-16 NKJV*

"Therefore the LORD will wait, that He may be gracious to you; And therefore He will be exalted, that He may have mercy on you. For the LORD is a God of justice; Blessed are all those who wait for Him." *Isaiah 30:18 NKJV*

"Then the LORD answered me and said: "Write the vision And make it plain on tablets, That he may run who reads it. For the vision is yet for an appointed time; But at the end it will speak, and it will not lie. Though it tarries, wait for it; Because it will surely come, It will not tarry." *Habakkuk 2:2-3 NKJV*

"The LORD is my portion," says my soul, "Therefore I hope in Him!" The LORD is good to those who wait for Him, To the soul who seeks Him. It is good that one should hope and wait quietly For the salvation of the LORD." *Lamentations 3:24-26 NKJV*

"Then she made a vow and said, "O LORD of hosts, if You will indeed look on the affliction of Your maidservant and remember me, and not forget Your maidservant, but will give Your maidservant a male child, then I will give him to the LORD all the days of his life, and no razor shall come upon his head."" *I Samuel 1:11 NKJV*

"Then Eli answered and said, "Go in peace, and the God of Israel grant your petition which you have asked of Him."" *I Samuel 1:17 NKJV*

"Are there any among the idols of the nations that can cause rain? Or can the heavens give showers? Are You not He, O LORD our God? Therefore we will wait for You, Since You have made all these." *Jeremiah 14:22 NKJV*

"Therefore I will look to the LORD; I will wait for the God of my salvation;

My God will hear me." *Micah 7:7 NKJV*

"Therefore be patient, brethren, until the coming of the Lord. See how the farmer waits for the precious fruit of the earth, waiting patiently for it until it receives the early and latter rain. You also be patient. Establish your hearts, for the coming of the Lord is at hand." *James 5:7-8 NKJV*

""Let your waist be girded and your lamps burning; and you yourselves be like men who wait for their master, when he will return from the wedding, that when he comes and knocks they may open to him immediately. Blessed are those servants whom the master, when he comes, will find watching. Assuredly, I say to you that he will gird himself and have them sit down to eat, and will come and serve them. And if he should come in the second watch, or come in the third watch, and find them so, blessed are those servants. But know this, that if the master of the house had known what hour the thief would come, he would have watched and not allowed his house to be broken into. Therefore you also be ready, for the Son of Man is coming at an hour you do not expect."" *Luke 12:35-40 NKJV*

"so that you come short in no gift, eagerly waiting for the revelation of our Lord Jesus Christ," *I Corinthians 1:7 NKJV*

"Therefore judge nothing before the time, until the Lord comes, who will both bring to light the hidden things of darkness and reveal the counsels of the hearts. Then each one's praise will come from God." *I Corinthians 4:5 NKJV*